Families

Parents

Rebecca Rissman

Heinemann Library
Chicago, Illinois

MW01153701

www.heinemannraintree.com
Visit our website to find out more information about Heinemann-Raintree books.

To order:
☎ Phone 888-454-2279
💻 Visit www.heinemannraintree.com to browse our catalog and order online.

© 2011 Heinemann Library
an imprint of Capstone Global Library, LLC
Chicago, Illinois

All rights reserved. No part of this publication may be reproduced or transmitted in any form or by any means, electronic or mechanical, including photocopying, recording, taping, or any information storage and retrieval system, without permission in writing from the publisher.

Edited by Rebecca Rissman and Catherine Veitch
Designed by Ryan Frieson
Picture research by Tracy Cummins
Originated by Capstone Global Library Ltd
Printed and bound in the United States of America, North Mankato, MN

14 13 12
10 9 8 7 6 5 4 3 2

Library of Congress Cataloging-in-Publication Data
Rissman, Rebecca.
  Parents / Rebecca Rissman.
    p. cm.—(Families)
  Includes bibliographical references and index.
  ISBN 978-1-4329-4659-3 (hc) — ISBN 978-1-4329-4667-8 (pb)
  1. Parents—Juvenile literature. 2. Families—Juvenile literature. I. Title.
  HQ755.8.R58 2011
  306.874—dc22   2010016995

072012
0067/93RP

Acknowledgments
We would like to thank the following for permission to reproduce photographs: Corbis pp. **9** (©Hans Neleman), **13** (©Terry Vine/Blend Images); Getty Images pp. **4** (Pankaj Shah), **5** (DK Stock/Kevin RL Hanson), **7** (Ben Bloom), **10** (Wang Leng), **11** (Dennie Cody), **12** (Jamie Chomas), **16** (Richard Schultz), **17** (Natalie Kauffman), **18** (Asia Images Group), **19** (Charlie Schuck), **21** (David Sacks), **23 b** (Wang Leng), **23 c** (Richard Schultz), **23 d** (Natalie Kauffman); istockphoto pp. **20** (©Alexander Shalamov), **22** (©Diane Labombarbe), **23 a** (©Alexander Shalamov); Photolibrary p. **6** (Picture Partners); Shutterstock pp. **8** (©Olga Lyubkina), **14** (©BlueOrange Studio), **15** (©Rob Marmion). Front cover photograph of a family of four reproduced with permission of Getty Images (Rhea Anna). Back cover photograph of a mother and baby reproduced with permission of Shutterstock (©BlueOrange Studio).

We would like to thank Anne Pezalla and Nancy Harris for their invaluable help in the preparation of this book.

Every effort has been made to contact copyright holders of any material reproduced in this book. Any omissions will be rectified in subsequent printings if notice is given to the publisher.

Contents

What Is a Family?

A family is a group of people.

The people in a family care for
each other.

All families are different.

All families are special.

What Are Families Like?

Some families like to be active.

They like to play sports.

Some families like to be quiet.

They like to read books.

Different Parents

Parents are adults who have children.

Parents can be male or female.

Male parents are called fathers.

Some children call their fathers "Dad."

Female parents are called mothers.
Some children call their mothers "Mom."

Some families have two parents.

Some families have one parent.

Some families do not have parents.
Other adults help care for the children.

Sometimes parents remarry.
Sometimes they become stepparents.

Stepparents care for the children of other parents.

Many parents live with their children.

Some parents live apart from their children.

Some parents adopt children.

The children join a new family.

Are there parents in your family?

Family Tree

Mother — You — Father

Picture Glossary

adopt join a new family.
Many families adopt children.

adult grown-up

remarry get married again.
Many parents remarry.

stepparent grown-up that cares for
children of other parents

Index

Note to Parents and Teachers

Before Reading

Explain to children that a family is a group of people who care for one another. Families can be very different. Most families include parents who care for the children. Some families have two parents, some have one parent, and some families include stepparents. Other families do not include parents. Other adults care for the children.

After Reading

- Talk to children about adoption. Explain that when parents adopt a child, they invite the child into their home to live. Some parents adopt one child. Other parents adopt more than one child.

- Ask children to draw a picture of their family and label the people in their drawing. Put these drawings up on display for everyone to enjoy!